THE OLYMPICS

GREAT OLYMPIC MOMENTS

HAYDN MIDDLETON

The Olympic spirit

The modern Olympic Games began in 1896. Since then the Games' organizers have tried to ensure that every competitor keeps to the true Olympic spirit. This spirit is based on fair play, international friendship, a love of sport purely for its own sake and the ideal that it is more important to take part than to win.

Heinemann
LIBRARY

First published in Great Britain by Heinemann Library,
Halley Court, Jordan Hill, Oxford OX2 8EJ,
a division of Reed Educational and Professional Publishing Ltd.
Heinemann is a registered trademark of Reed Educational & Professional Publishing Limited.

OXFORD MELBOURNE AUCKLAND
JOHANNESBURG BLANTYRE GABORONE
IBADAN PORTSMOUTH NH (USA) CHICAGO

Designed by AMR
Originated by Dot Gradations
Printed in Hong Kong/China

03 02 01 00
10 9 8 7 6 5 4 3 2

ISBN 0 431 05920 9

British Library Cataloguing in Publication Data
Middleton, Haydn
  Great olympic moments. – (The olympics)
  1.Olympic games – Juvenile literature 2.Olympics – Records
  – Juvenile literature
  I.Title
  796.4·8

Acknowledgements
The Publishers would like to thank the following for permission to reproduce photographs:
Allsport: pp6, 7, 8, 9, 10, 11, 12, 13, 14, 15, 18, 20, 21, 22, 24, 25, 26, 28, 29; Colorsport: pp16,
19; Corbis/Bettmann: p23; Empics: p17; Hulton Getty: p27.

Cover photograph reproduced with permission of Bob Martin, Allsport.

Every effort has been made to contact copyright holders of any material reproduced in this
book. Any omissions will be rectified in subsequent printings if notice is given to the Publisher.

For more information about Heinemann Library books, or to order, please phone
++44 (0)1865 888066, or send a fax to ++44 (0)1865 314091. You can visit our website
at www.heinemann.co.uk.

Any words appearing in the text in bold, **like this**, are explained in the Glossary.

Contents

Introduction

The modern Olympics began in 1896. Every Games since then has been lit up by marvellous sporting moments. The Olympic motto is '*Citius, Altius, Fortius*'– which is Latin for 'Swifter, Higher, Stronger'. In this book you can read about men and women – runners, jumpers, swimmers, gymnasts, skiers, footballers – who made that motto a reality in their own events. Sometimes they achieved success with style and ease. Sometimes they fought against terrific odds to come out on top. All of them won lasting, world-wide fame.

The joy of taking part

For competitors and spectators alike, nothing quite compares with the thrill of an Olympic final. Britain's Sebastian Coe knows that as well as anyone. In 1980 and again in 1984 he won the 1500 metres gold medal. 'There may be championships galore,' he wrote later, '... but to every young athlete who tied on his or her first pair of spikes in a draughty clubhouse in Sheffield, or a high-school trackside in Baltimore, or a corrugated-roofed changing room in a Nairobi suburb, it is the Olympic final that matters.'

But the Olympic Games have a second, longer and unofficial, motto. It was adapted from an American bishop's sermon in 1908, and it describes what could be called the true 'Olympic spirit': 'The most important thing in the Olympic Games is not to win but to take part, just as the most important thing in life is not the triumph but the struggle. The essential thing is not to have conquered but to have fought well.'

How many of these great Olympic champions can you name? You will meet them again later in this book.

4

This might seem hard to believe nowadays. In our world, winning often seems to mean everything and coming second is often portrayed in the **media** as failure. But it need not be that way, as this little Olympic story shows....

From me to you

Czech distance-runner Emil Zatopek was one of the greatest Olympians of all. In the early 1950s no one could match him, and at the Helsinki Games of 1952 he won three gold medals. Then in the 1960s another magnificent distance-runner emerged: Ron Clarke of Australia. Everyone knew Clarke was the world's best and he had the records to prove it. But although he gave his all at Tokyo in 1964 and at Mexico City in 1968 – and helped to make both Games so memorable – he came away without a single Olympic victory.

On his way back to Australia in 1968, he stopped over in Europe to see his old friend Emil Zatopek. On parting from him, Zatopek gave him a small gift, which Clarke opened only when he got home. Inside the wrapping was Zatopek's 10,000 metres gold medal from 1952. As Sebastian Coe points out: 'Zatopek, the kindest of men, well knew the important difference between failure and not winning. In that sense Ron Clarke had not failed, and the Olympic Games were richer for him.' In the pages that follow, you will meet many others who have truly enriched the Olympics....

VENUES OF THE MODERN OLYMPIC GAMES		
Year	Summer Games	Winter Games
1896	Athens, Greece	–
1900	Paris, France	–
1904	St Louis, USA	–
1908	London, UK	–
1912	Stockholm, Sweden	–
1916	Games not held	–
1920	Antwerp, Belgium	–
1924	Paris, France	Chamonix, France
1928	Amsterdam, Netherlands	St Moritz, Switzerland
1932	Los Angeles, USA	Lake Placid, USA
1936	Berlin, Germany	Garmisch-Partenkirchen, Germany
1940	Games not held	Games not held
1944	Games not held	Games not held
1948	London, UK	St Moritz, Switzerland
1952	Helsinki, Finland	Oslo, Norway
1956	Melbourne, Australia	Cortina, Italy
1960	Rome, Italy	Squaw Valley, USA
1964	Tokyo, Japan	Innsbruck, Austria
1968	Mexico City, Mexico	Grenoble, France
1972	Munich, West Germany	Sapporo, Japan
1976	Montreal, Canada	Innsbruck, Austria
1980	Moscow, **USSR**	Lake Placid, USA
1984	Los Angeles, USA	Sarajevo, Yugoslavia (now Bosnia)
1988	Seoul, South Korea	Calgary, Canada
1992	Barcelona, Spain	Albertville, France
1994	–	Lillehammer, Norway
1996	Atlanta, USA	–
1998	–	Nagano, Japan
2000	Sydney, Australia	–

The Winter Games were not held until 1924. Since 1992 the Summer and Winter Games have been held on a staggered two-year schedule.

The fastest men in the world

For many sports fans, nothing can beat the sheer excitement of the two great Olympic sprint races – over 100 metres and 200 metres. The first Olympic 100 metres champion was an American, Thomas Burke, who won the 1896 race in Athens in 12.0 seconds. (To show how times change – 100 years later, at Atlanta, Canadian Donovan Bailey won the gold medal in a time of 9.84 seconds!)

Until 1924, Americans then won every 100 metres title except one. All these winners were white men but more and more black athletes were going to American high schools and colleges, to get the necessary coaching to become great Olympians. At Los Angeles in 1932 Thomas 'Eddie' Tolan, a black sprinter from the University of Michigan, won gold in both the 100 metres and 200 metres. Four years later, his successor as Olympic sprint champion was perhaps *the* all-time great....

Enter Jesse Owens

By the time of the 11th Games in 1936, James 'Jesse' Owens was already a living legend. The year before, at an American championship, he had broken five world records and equalled a sixth – all in the space of 45 minutes.

News of this fabulous feat stunned the world. But surely he would have a hard job living up to everyone's expectations at the Berlin Olympics?

The magnificent Jesse Owens. In 1936 he was asked for the secret of his success by a London reporter. 'I let my feet spend as little time as possible on the ground,' Owens replied. 'From the air, fast down, and from the ground, fast up. My foot is only a fraction of the time on the track.'

In later years, to make ends meet, he allowed promoters to put on exhibitions where he raced against horses, dogs and motorcycles.

6

He would also have to run and jump there in a very odd atmosphere. Germany's ruling **Nazi** Party was trying hard to convince anyone who would listen that athletes from the white German 'master race' were 'superior' to those from any other. They saw the Olympic Games as an opportunity to demonstrate their racist theory.

The 'master race' was one thing. The 'master racer' was quite another. Jesse Owens proved himself to be unbeatable at the 100 metres, the 200 metres, the long jump and the sprint relay – and in the words of one rival, he made it all look as easy and inevitable as 'water running downhill'. At the time, few people would have guessed that Owens' four-gold-medal achievement would ever be equalled at a later Games. But it was, in 1984 – by another black American hero.

Carl Lewis of the USA – not just a world-beating sprinter but a fabulous long-jumper too. At Atlanta in 1996, he won the Olympic long jump for the *fourth* time.

From crutches to glory

Carl Lewis was small as a child but at the age of fifteen he began to grow – so fast that he had to use crutches for three weeks while his body adjusted. His body adjusted very well. In 1984 at Los Angeles, he won gold in exactly the same four events as Jesse Owens. Owens had won the 100 metres in 10.3 seconds. Lewis won in 9.92 seconds and by a margin of eight feet – the widest in Olympic history.

In 1988 at Seoul he retained his 100 metres and long jump titles – which no man had ever done before – but managed only silver in the 200 metres. He was not finished yet, though. In Barcelona in 1992 he picked up his seventh and eighth gold medals in the long jump and the sprint relay. Unlike Owens, Lewis never had to race against horses in later life. By the age of 23 he was already earning $1 million a year from **endorsements** – even though he was still classed as an **amateur**!

Fabulous Finns

The Olympic all-time medals table is topped by the USA. You might have expected that. It is a big, rich country which has always taken the training of its athletes very seriously. Its **Cold War** rival the **USSR** – in second place – turned the making of Olympic champions into a kind of industry. Then come several European nations, like Germany and Italy, with a long history of sporting excellence. But just behind them is a rather surprising country: Finland.

Lasse Viren (in front): one of a long line of great Finnish distance runners.

The driving force of *sisu*

Between 1912 and 1936 Finland's track athletes won 24 gold medals. This was an extraordinary achievement for a nation which numbers only five million people *today*. A second great age of Olympic success opened up for the Finns at Munich in 1972 – and then, as before, they did best at long and middle-distance running.

Why was this? No one can say for sure. But the Finns themselves talk of a national characteristic called *sisu* – a single-minded mixture of pride and guts and the sheer will to win. Perhaps it had something to do with that.

At the 1912 Games in Stockholm, there was not even an independent country called Finland. It was still a part of the Russian Empire, so its athletes had to run under the Russian flag. That did not stop smiling Hannes Kolemainen – a vegetarian bricklayer – from winning the 10,000 metres, the cross-country race and the 5000 metres.

Finnish flyers

From 1920 to 1928, carpenter's son Paavo Nurmi was so far ahead of his rivals that his main challenge came from beating his own previous time. In fact he ran *carrying* a stopwatch, to improve his pace judgement even further! He won nine Olympic gold medals and broke 22 official world records in distances ranging from 1500 metres to 20,000 metres. And when he left the scene, other distance-runners kept Finland high in the medals table until the outbreak of World War Two. Then, amazingly, from 1948 to 1972 the Finns did not win a single Olympic title. The man who changed all that was another **phenomenon** of the track: Lasse Viren.

This 23-year-old policeman won his first gold medal at Munich the hard way. In the middle of the 10,000 metres final Viren stumbled and fell. One of his main rivals, Muhammad Gammoudi tripped on him, crashed to the ground, and left the race shortly after. Viren, though, got up and carried on – all the way to the gold medal, in a brand new world record time of 27 minutes 36.35 seconds. He then won the 5000 metres too. And at Montreal four years later he not only repeated his double-gold performance, he came within a whisker of winning the marathon as well! If any Finnish athlete had *sisu* to spare, it was Lasse Viren.

Finnish athletes have excelled in the javelin, as well as long-distance running. In the men's event, Finns have won seven Olympic titles since World War One.

In the women's event, Ilse 'Tiina' Lillak won the 1983 World Championship with a last-round throw of 69 m 57 cm – a new world record. Only an injury to her right foot stopped her from winning the Olympic title at Los Angeles in 1984 too.

Tiny gymnastic giants

The sport of gymnastics has figured in every modern Games since 1896. But, as in most Olympic sports, women's competitions took longer to arrive than men's. At Amsterdam in 1928 the first women's gymnastic team event took place. Then, in 1952, women's individual apparatus was introduced. So the stage was set for some of the most memorable Olympic champions of all – many of them coming from the countries of eastern Europe.

Eastern European gold

At the 1972 Games, the world met 'The Munchkin of Munich' – an **elfin** seventeen-year-old gymnast from the **USSR** called Olga Korbut. She was only 150 centimetres tall and weighed just 39 kilograms. Her mischievous smile entranced millions. She was also popular with the judges, who awarded her three gold medals even though some experts questioned her technique. Her team-mate, nineteen-year-old Lyudmila Turischeva, won the all-round title. Four years later another young Soviet gymnast, Nelli Kim, received two perfect scores of '10' for her performances. Even so, she did not manage to win the all-round crown.

Olga Korbut – darling of the world's **media** at Munich in 1972. When she went for a walk during the Games, buses stopped so that passengers could get out and ask for autographs. On returning home to Grodno in the USSR, she got so much fan mail that a clerk was employed just to deal with letters for her.

The champion that year in Montreal was Romania's awesome Nadia Comaneci. Only fourteen years of age, she had been trained as a gymnast since the age of six. She scored '10's from all seven judges on both the parallel bars and the balance beam. Unprepared for such a gymnastic genius, the electronic scoreboard could show nothing higher than 9.95. And for Comaneci's performance it registered only 1.00. But she knew she had achieved perfection. Four years later, as a 'veteran' of eighteen, she dazzled again at Moscow, and her final haul of Olympic medals was nine – five of them gold.

Nadia Comaneci, the star of the 1976 Games. At press conferences in Montreal, journalists asked the shy fourteen-year-old what was her greatest wish. 'I want to go home,' she replied. They also asked her if she had any plans for retirement!

The older generation

Between 1956 and 1964, USSR gymnast Larissa Latynina won eighteen Olympic medals, more than any other Olympian in history. At the 1956 and 1960 Games, she won the all-round crown for woman gymnasts – a feat equalled only by Vera Caslavska of Czechoslovakia in 1964 and 1968. Whereas Caslavska was famous for artistic expression, Latynina was technically superb. At Rome in 1960 she competed as a young mother, having taken time out to give birth to a daughter, Tatiana – who went on to become a well-known ballet dancer (her mother's own childhood dream).

Leaps of the century

Someone once said that Olympic records are like piecrusts – they are meant to be broken. Since 1896, more than 50 per cent of the finals of **track and field** events have been won with a record-breaking performance. The figure for swimming is over 70 per cent. In some Olympic events, however, records tend to stand for a very long time. In the case of the men's long jump, it can seem like an eternity.

At Berlin in 1936 super-athlete Jesse Owens took the long jump gold medal, setting a new Olympic record of 8.06 m. But he could not beat the world record he had set the year before. On that day in Michigan, just before he jumped for the first time, an announcer told the crowd: 'Jesse Owens will now attempt a new long jump world's record.' And he did it, with a leap of 8.13 m! His record stood until fellow-American Ralph Boston broke it … in 1960.

Bob Beamon makes his massive leap at the Mexico City Games of 1968. He jumped beyond the range of the officials' state-of-the-art measuring device, so an old-fashioned steel tape had to be called for.

Dizzy heights for long-jumpers

Before the Mexico Games of 1968, everyone was talking about the city's great **altitude**. The thin air, they thought, would surely have a bad effect on the breathing of long-distance runners. But no one predicted the *good* effect it would have on specialists in the more explosive events – like the long jump.

The three medallists from Tokyo in 1964 – Lynn Davies (GB), Ralph Boston (USA) and Igor Ter-Ovanesyan (**USSR**) – were all competing again. Each was in good enough form to win the gold. But an outsider struggled through the qualifying round to compete against them in the final.

He was a 190-centimetre-tall, 22-year-old New Yorker called Bob Beamon, who could run like the wind but had great trouble in hitting the take-off board right. Scheduled to jump fourth among the seventeen finalists, with his first leap he took long-jumping into a new dimension. After a perfect take-off he sailed through the air at almost his own height, then hit the sand so hard that he bounced back up and landed outside the pit.

'You have destroyed this event'

How far had Beamon gone? The electronic scoreboard showed a distance of 8.90 metres. It was stupendous. But until the metric measurement was converted into feet and inches, the jumper himself did not fully realize what he had done. No one in history had ever achieved a 28-feet jump. And *still* no one had – because the gangling American had bypassed 28 feet altogether and cleared *29* feet, two and a half inches! No one could hope to beat that. A dazed Lynn Davies said to the new champion, 'You have destroyed this event.' (He was not quite right. In 1991, Mike Powell finally surpassed Beamon's world-record mark in a non-Olympic competition.) But the freak jump of 1968 still stands as an Olympic record.

High jump flops

Unlike the long jump, the high jump did not figure in the ancient Greek Games, but in modern times it is often a breathtakingly exciting event. American Dick Fosbury changed its nature forever in Mexico City when he won gold with his new head-first and backwards style of clearing the bar. The 'Fosbury Flop' later became the standard style for high-jumpers, but in 1968 it looked very risky. Fosbury's coach warned, 'If kids imitate Fosbury he will wipe out an entire generation of jumpers because they will all have broken necks.'

Amazing Africans

Until 1960 no black African athlete had won a **track-and-field** gold medal. That all changed at the Rome Olympics, thanks to an Ethiopian bodyguard with the initials AB – Abebe Bikila – and he made winning the marathon look as easy as ABC.

Marathon marvel

The 1960 marathon was the first to be staged at night, when the temperature was cooler. It was also the first to start and end outside the stadium. And it was the third time Abebe Bikila had run a marathon in his life. He won – barefoot – in a time of 2 hours 15 minutes 16.2 seconds. And his biggest challenge close to the tape came from a motor-scooter rider who lurched on to the course by mistake!

Four years later, Abebe proved that his victory was no flash in the pan. Only 40 days before the Tokyo marathon he had his appendix removed. But he still finished first in a time of 2 hours 12 minutes 11.2 seconds – the fastest ever recorded. He even ran a lap of honour before Britain's Basil Heatley appeared in the stadium to take the silver.

Kenyan policeman Kipchoge Keino, the undisputed track star of the 1968 Games. As a boy he had run fifteen miles to and from school each day.

Africans at altitude

At Mexico City in 1968 another Ethiopian, 36-year-old Mamo Wolde, won the marathon. More than an hour after he broke the tape, John Akhwari of Tanzania entered the stadium. He had hurt himself badly in a fall but struggled on through the pain. 'My country did not send me 7000 miles to start the race,' he said afterwards. 'They sent me 7000 miles to finish it.'

Many African athletes lived and trained at high **altitudes**, so the Mexico City Games – held at more than 2000 metres above sea level – held no terrors for them. At every distance from 1500 metres to the marathon, African runners took gold. In the 5000 metres and 10,000 metres all three medallists came from Africa. In the first of those races, uncoached Kenyan Kipchoge 'Kip' Keino lost by a hair's breadth to Tunisia's Muhammad Gammoudi. In the 1500 metres he went one place better – even though he had to run to the stadium before the race after being caught in a traffic jam.

Keino was up against world-record-holder Jim Ryun of the USA. He had also been suffering from violent stomach pains. You would not have known it as, at the finish, Keino took the gold by beating Ryun by 20 metres, the largest-ever margin of victory in this event. At Munich four years later Keino was beaten into second place in the 1500 metres by Pekka Vasala of Finland. But he decided to enter the 3000 metres steeplechase too, as a challenge. In this event – featuring 28 hurdles and seven water jumps – Keino had little experience, and he admitted that he jumped 'like an animal'. But he was still good enough to win the gold medal, and set an Olympic record time of 8 minutes 23.6 seconds in beating everyone else in sight.

At Barcelona in 1992 the women's 10,000 m was a race to remember. After the 6000 m mark, South African Elana Meyer took the lead. Derartu Tulu of Ethiopia went with her. Soon these two were so far ahead that no one else could catch them. Lap after lap Tulu ran just behind Meyer. Then with 420 m to go, she eased in front, stormed away and won by a full 30 m.

For the first time ever, a black African woman had won an Olympic medal. And Meyer's silver was South Africa's first medal since her country had been banned after the 1960 Games. They set off hand in hand for a shared victory lap.

Soccer stars

The soccer World Cup began in 1930. Until then, the winners of the Olympic soccer tournament could rightly be called the champions of the world. Only five countries entered the first full tournament, at the 1908 Games, and it was won by England. The 1920 final between host nation Belgium and Czechoslovakia was a bad-tempered affair. It ended with the Czech team – trailing 2–0 and feeling that the referee was favouring the home side – simply walking off the field in the second half!

True world champions

At the 1924 Games in Paris, many Europeans were able to watch a dazzling South American team for the first time. That team was Uruguay, and they took the tournament by storm, beating Switzerland 3–0 in the final to take the gold.

OLYMPIC SOCCER CHAMPIONS
Since the first full Olympic soccer tournament in 1908, these have been the winners:
1908 England
1912 England
1920 Belgium
1924 Uruguay
1928 Uruguay
1936 Italy
1948 Sweden
1952 Hungary
1956 USSR
1960 Yugoslavia
1964 Hungary
1968 Hungary
1972 Poland
1976 East Germany
1980 Czechoslovakia
1984 France
1988 USSR
1992 Spain
1996 Nigeria

In 1996 the first women's Olympic tournament was held – won by the USA.

The last Olympic champions who could also be called true world champions were Hungary in 1952. Featuring stars like Hidegkuti, Koscis and Puskas (on the left), they scored 20 goals and conceded only two in winning the 1952 tournament.

Virtually the same team then played in the 1954 World Cup Final against West Germany. Earlier in the competition they had already thrashed the Germans 8–3, yet to everyone's amazement they managed to lose the final 2–3.

Four years later, in Amsterdam, the Uruguayans were back – accompanied by fellow-South Americans Argentina. The Argentinians thrashed the USA 11–2, beat Belgium 6–3, then crushed Egypt 6–0 on route to the final. There they met … Uruguay! After the first match ended in a draw, Uruguay won the replay 2–1 to retain their Olympic title. Few could doubt that they were the best team in the world. When the first World Cup was held – in Uruguay – in 1930, they won that too.

The US women's soccer team, who won the first Olympic gold medal in their sport in 1996. They are shown here beating Norway in the semi-finals.

In 1936 in Berlin recent World-Cup-winners Italy also won the gold. But by that time, so many of the world's footballers were **professional** that many nations had to send under-strength squads to the **amateur** Olympics. And during the **Cold War** period, the **Communist** countries of eastern Europe dominated the tournament, combining skill with strong government support.

Professionals allowed in

After 1976, professional players who had not competed in World Cup games were allowed to take part in the Olympics. Soccer at the Games continued to draw in huge crowds. In 1984 and 1988 more spectators watched soccer than any other event, including athletics. Then in 1992, at Barcelona, the rules changed again: the Olympic soccer tournament became the official competition for all the world's under-23-year-old teams.

Repeat performances

To win a gold medal in any Olympic event is a supreme achievement. To go back four years later and win again is quite staggering. But to be the Olympic champion a third time, a *fourth* time, that seems almost unbelievable. It takes a very special person indeed to be the world's best for a period of sixteen years. Yet it has happened.…

One-man gold rushes

Ray Ewry of the USA won a record ten gold medals in the now-discontinued 'standing jumps' between 1900 and 1908 – in spite of the fact that Ewry had suffered from polio as a boy. Russian triple-jumper Viktor Saneyev won his event in 1968, 1972 and 1976. Then in 1980, at the age of 34, he failed by only 11 centimetres to add a fourth gold medal to his career total.

But by then, one man had already achieved that stupendous feat. He was Paul Elvstrom of Denmark, who won his four consecutive gold medals in the Finn class of the yachting competitions between 1948 and 1960. At the Helsinki Games of 1952, he was already so many points ahead that he did not have to race on the last day. But he entered anyway – and won that race too!

British oarsman Steve Redgrave has won gold medals at four Olympic Games in a row. The official magazine of the International Olympic Committee pronounced him 'Rower of the Century'.

After winning the coxless pairs in Atlanta with Matthew Pinsent, he publicly asked his wife to shoot him if he tried to go on rowing. She must have missed. He is now in training to challenge for a *fifth* consecutive gold medal at the Sydney Games in the year 2000!

The ultimate competitor

The only athlete ever to win the same Olympic **track-and-field** event four times is discus-thrower Al Oerter in 1956, 1960, 1964 and 1968. When he won his first gold with a new Olympic record, the truth did not sink in until he was up on the victory **rostrum**. Then his knees buckled and he almost fell off.

He had plenty of time to get used to standing at that dizzy height. But Oerter was more than just a great thrower, he was a great *competitor*. Three times he had to beat the current world-record holder to win gold. Three times he produced a lifetime-best throw to set the winning mark. And at Tokyo in 1964, he injured his lower ribs so badly while practising, that doctors told him to forget about competing. But it took more than that to stop him. With his fifth throw, as he doubled up in pain he set a new Olympic record to win the event. 'These are the Olympics,' the hero explained afterwards. 'You die for them.'

Britain's Francis 'Daley' Thompson, who won the gruelling **decathlon** twice, in 1980 and again in 1984. His points total in Los Angeles has not been beaten at any Games since then. British Olympic 800 m champion Steve Ovett called the decathlon 'nine Mickey Mouse events followed by a slow 1500 metres'. But Thompson's 1984 times and distances would have won him *individual* gold medals at the 1912 Games in the 100 m, long jump, 400 m, 110 m hurdles, discus, pole vault and javelin. Mickey would have been delighted!

Pick of the pool

Greg Louganis – springboard and platform king

Only two divers have won the springboard *and* platform events at two different Olympic Games. The first was Patricia McCormick of the USA in 1952 and 1956 – and she won the latter pair of golds only five months after giving birth to a son. The second was fellow-American Greg Louganis in 1984 and 1988. Louganis had a tough early life. He recovered from being a teenage **alcoholic**, but he was so good at diving that he qualified for the 1976 Games when aged only sixteen. On the springboard in 1984 his winning margin of 94 points was the biggest in Olympic history.

Four years later in Seoul, he hit his head on the springboard during the preliminary round. But still he went on to win the final. Then he had to face fourteen-year-old **prodigy** Xiong Ni from China in the platform final. It was neck and neck until Louganis' last dive: known as the 'Dive of Death' because two men had died trying to make it. Louganis survived – and won.

Johnny Weissmuller – king of the water, lord of the apes

As a child, Romanian-born American Johnny Weissmuller was believed to have heart problems. But he grew up to become the first person to swim the 100 m in less than a minute (in 1922). At the Paris Games of 1924, he won three gold medals, and he went on to keep his 100 m title at Amsterdam in 1928. His style was extremely relaxed: 'I didn't tense up,' he explained. After retiring from the pool, he took up acting and became a famous Hollywood Tarzan, starring in many films. Three other Olympic medallists also played that movie role!

Mark Spitz – most-golden Olympian

American swimmer Mark Spitz began his glittering Olympic career at Mexico City in 1968 – and went home with four medals: two golds for relays and a silver and a bronze for individual events. That was pretty good. But at Munich four years later he rewrote the record books. He won *seven* gold medals there in all, the most ever won at a single Games. More astonishing still, he won every gold medal in a new world-record time. His father would have been pleased. 'Swimming isn't everything,' he had told Mark as a boy, 'winning is.'

Dawn Fraser – Australia's greatest Olympian?

Dawn Fraser was only nineteen years old when she won her first Olympic 100 m title, in her native Australia in 1956. She did it in a world record time of 1 min 02 secs too – not bad for someone who had been sickly and **asthmatic** as a child, and who was swimming in her first international tournament. At Rome in 1960, having already set a new world record, she successfully defended her Olympic 100 m title.

In 1964, the year of the Tokyo Games, she was terribly badly injured in a car crash but managed to get fit for the Olympics. At 27 years of age now, her team-mates called her 'Granny'! But experience paid off in the 100 m final, when she beat fifteen-year-old American Sharon Stouder to win again. No other Olympic swimmer, male or female, had ever won the same individual event three times running. She celebrated by trying to steal a 'souvenir' flag from the Japanese Emperor's palace in the middle of the night. She was caught and arrested, but the Emperor saw the joke and gave her the flag anyway.

Supreme strongmen

Alexander Medved – Soviet wrestling sensation

Russian freestyle wrestler Alexander Medved has been called the greatest wrestler of the 20th century – and even of the past 2000 years! The mighty wrestlers of ancient times would probably have found this nimble bear of a man hard to beat. As a light-heavyweight and then as a super-heavyweight, he won three Olympic titles between 1964 and 1972. He also won ten world championships in three weight divisions between 1962 and 1972. Rarely weighing more than his opponent, he won by speed, power and intelligence.

Naim Suleymanoglu – Turkey's 'Pocket Hercules'

Featherweight weightlifter Naim Suleymanoglu was born in Bulgaria but his family was Turkish. Although not quite 150 cm tall, he was immensely strong. At the age of fourteen he came within 2.5 kg of breaking the *adult* world record for combined lifts, and by the age of sixteen he was lifting three times his own body weight. In 1984 he was too young to compete for Bulgaria at the Los Angeles Olympics. But four years later he did appear – in the *Turkish* team. (In 1986 he had **defected**; and for a fee of over $1 million from the Turkish government, the government of Bulgaria let him change his nationality.)

In Seoul he won Turkey's first gold medal for 20 years. Girls had used to laugh at him for being so short. Now he was a national sex symbol! He wanted to retire while still at the top but was persuaded to keep competing. This turned out to be a good idea. He won in Barcelona and again in Atlanta, thus becoming weightlifting's first triple Olympic champion in three successive Games.

Cassius Clay – the best *and* the prettiest (or so he said!)

No boxer ever talked a better fight – or fought one – than Cassius Marcellus Clay – winner of the light-heavyweight gold at Rome in 1960. Eighteen at the time, he was so proud of his medal that he wore it all the time, even sleeping with it, so that the gold plating began to come off. He later turned **professional** and won the world heavyweight championship in 1964, before converting to Islam and changing his name to Muhammad Ali. A uniquely talented sportsman, he became one of the world's most famous people during the 1960s and 1970s.

Yasuhiro Yamashita – Japan's big fridge!

At almost 180 cm in height and weighing 125 kg, judo open champion Yasuhiro Yamashita from Japan was described by one opponent as 'a refrigerator with a head on top'. After losing in the final of the Japanese Student Championships in 1977, he did not lose one of his next 194 matches at national and international level! He won his Olympic title in 1984 with such a bad leg injury that his opponent had to help him up to the top step to receive his gold medal.

The flying housewife

After the 1948 Olympic Games in London, a Dutch athlete called Fanny Blankers-Koen was paraded through Amsterdam in an open coach drawn by four grey horses. Great crowds flocked to see and cheer her. 'All I've done is run fast,' said the 30-year-old mother of two. 'I don't quite see why people should make such a fuss

about that.' As usual, Mrs Blankers-Koen was being far too modest. She had just become the undisputed star of the London Games – and what a roller-coaster ride it had been for her there!

Games to brighten the gloom

Between 1936 and 1948 – thanks to World War Two – there were no Olympic Games. The War ended in 1945, but so much damage had been done that life was hardly back to normal in Britain by 1948. Food and clothes were still being **rationed**, many houses had been bombed to rubble – and yet London had to stage the next Games. The organizers made the best of the situation, spending only £600,000, trying to ignore the torrential rain, housing the male athletes in Army camps and the women in colleges. One of these women was Fanny Blankers-Koen of the Netherlands.

At Berlin in 1936, eighteen-year-old Fanny had seemed to have a glittering Olympic future. But when the 1940 and 1944 Games were cancelled, she had no chance to prove herself at the top. By 1948, aged 30, some experts thought she was past her peak. Jack Crump, the British athletes' team manager, was one of them. Fanny was 'too old to make the grade', he sniffed.

Over the course of eight days she had four events in which to prove him wrong: the 100 metres, the 80 metres hurdles, the 200 metres and the 4 × 100 metres relay.

Good as gold (× four)

Her first event was the 100 metres. She romped home, through the mud, in the final to win in a time (11.5 seconds) that equalled her own world record. The 80 metres hurdles came next. After a poor start, and then hitting the fifth hurdle, she lurched over the line neck-and-neck with Britain's Maureen Gardner. No one knew who had won. As the runners awaited the result, the band suddenly began to play the British national anthem. Did that mean Gardner had won? No, it was to mark the arrival of the British royal family in the stadium! When the result was announced, Fanny had her second gold medal.

Now the pressure began to build on this great athlete who was lighting up the Games. There was so much talk of her winning a hat-trick of gold medals, that she broke down and nearly pulled out of the 200 metres altogether. Her husband and coach persuaded her to run – and she finished with the biggest-ever winning margin in a women's 200 metres final.

Three events, three golds – and the 4 × 100 metres relay was still to come. Fanny ran the last leg and when she took the baton, it did not look good. The Dutch team was lying fourth. Surely she could not pass three runners over so short a distance? *As if!* Fanny broke the tape to become the first woman to win four **track-and-field** golds – and all in the same Games too. When she got home, her neighbours gave her a bicycle, 'so she won't have to run so much'.

You can't catch Zatopek

Some Olympic champions do not just win, they win in *style*. The star of the 1952 Games in Helsinki was no such stylist. According to one watcher, he ran 'like a man who had just been stabbed in the heart'. It was also said about him that 'he does everything wrong except win'. But no one could deny this awkward-looking runner's brilliance. Emil Zatopek was an all-time great.

Going for gold (× three)

Czech army officer Zatopek arrived in Helsinki in 1952 as the reigning Olympic champion at 10,000 metres. In 1948 he had also won a silver medal in the 5000 metres. But now he was 30 years old, and he had not been on top form before the Games. Nevertheless, he planned to compete in a *third* event within eight days in Helsinki: the marathon. He had never run a marathon before, but he believed his tough training methods would stand him in good stead.

Emil Zatopek, the incomparable Czech distance-runner. Between 1948 and 1954, he won 38 10,000 m races in a row – often by huge margins. Years later, he was asked why he looked so pained when he ran. 'I was not talented enough to run and smile at the same time,' he replied.

His first event was the 10,000 metres. The rest of the field was strong, but no one else could live with Zatopek's blistering pace. He won by about 100 metres. Next up was the 5000 metres: heats first, then the final – which turned out to be one of the most exciting Olympic races ever. Usually in the last lap, Zatopek simply burned off most of his challengers. This time, soon after he kicked for home, three runners stormed past *him*. This had never happened to him before.

With 250 metres to go, Herbert Schade of Germany, Britain's Chris Chataway and France's Alain Mimoun looked like sharing out the medals between them. Desperately Zatopek tried to catch up. With 180 metres to go all four runners were in a line across the track. The head of the one on the outside was rolling in agony, his arms were thrashing, his chest was heaving: Emil Zatopek – and 180 metres further on, he breasted the tape to win gold.

Zatopek with his wife Dana. Between them they won four Olympic golds in 1952.

'Fast enough for you?'

Later that afternoon, Zatopek heard that his wife, Dana, had just won a gold medal in the javelin. 'At present,' he joked with reporters, 'the score of the contest in the Zatopek family is 2–1. This result is too close. To restore some prestige I will try to improve on the margin – in the marathon race.' He did it….

After 15 kilometres, he was in the lead alongside Britain's Jim Peters. Six weeks before, Peters had run the fastest marathon in history. Zatopek, of course, had never run a marathon in his life. He turned to Peters and asked in perfect English: 'The pace, is it fast enough?' Peters had started too quickly, and now he felt exhausted. But he did not want Zatopek to know that, so he replied, 'No, it's too slow.' Zatopek thought about this, then raced ahead – to a stunning victory.

Zatopek's triple-gold haul in Helsinki was a magnificent achievement. No one has ever repeated it. But as the story on page 5 shows, Zatopek was not just a brilliant runner and racer, he was a true Olympian too.

Winter wonders

Sonja Henie – child skating star to film star

Norway's Sonja Henie was the greatest female figure skater in the world for more than a decade — and she remains the most successful, individual, woman skater in Olympic history. At the first Winter Olympics in 1924 she took part as an eleven-year-old. She won no medals at Chamonix, but thanks in part to seven hours of training each day, she never lost a competition after the age of thirteen. The winner of ten figure-skating world championships in a row, she was also the Olympic gold medallist in 1928, 1932 and 1936. Her **repertoire** was breathtaking, including a whirl with up to 80 spins.

In later life she followed a career in the movies, becoming a huge and fabulously wealthy star in the USA. Someone once said, however, that her acting skills were 'on a par with Charles Laughton's figure skating'. (Charles Laughton was a rather stout actor whose famous film roles included King Henry VIII of England and the Hunchback of Notre-Dame.)

Jean-Claude Killy – 'Killympic hero'

The star of the 1968 Winter Olympics at Grenoble was Alpine-skier Jean-Claude Killy. In the downhill event, in the slalom and also in the giant slalom, the 24-year-old Frenchman turned in gold-medal-winning performances. Like Torvill and Dean in Britain, he became an immensely popular hero in his own country; and after helping to organize the 1992 Winter Games he joined the International Olympic Committee in 1995.

Cool runnings

Most Winter Olympic teams come from countries where there is plenty of ice and snow. But at Albertville in 1992, there was a four-man bobsleigh team from … Jamaica! The Jamaicans did not win a medal, but it was a great achievement to qualify for the Games in the first place. The Walt Disney Corporation certainly thought so. They made a successful film about the team, *Cool Runnings*.

Eric Heiden – clean sweep speed skater

At the opening of the 1980 Winter Olympics in Lake Placid, USA, the Olympic oath was taken by Eric Heiden, the 21-year-old American speed skater. He stayed in the headlines by making a clean sweep of the five speed-skating gold medals, all in Olympic record times – and in the 10,000 m he set a new world record. Just for good measure, his sister Beth also won a bronze in the 3000 m event for women.

Torvill and Dean – incomparable ice dancers

By the time of the 1984 Games in Sarajevo, Britain's Jayne Torvill and Christopher Dean had already been the world ice-dance champions for three years. Their performances at the Olympics then took their sport to a new level of achievement. For their interpretation of Ravel's *Bolero*, all nine judges awarded them the maximum '6' points for artistic presentation. In the whole competition, they gained twelve '6's out of a possible eighteen.

Glossary

alcoholic person addicted to drinking alcohol

altitude height above sea level

amateur someone who competes for fun, rather than as a job, and who is unpaid

asthmatic suffering form asthma, a disease that affects a person's breathing

Cold War period, after World War Two, of unfriendly relations between USA and USSR, which never quite became head-to-head conflict

Communist the idea that a single, ruling political party can provide for all its people better than if they are left to make their own decisions and keep their own homes, land and businesses. The USSR became the first Communist state in 1917. After World War Two, the USSR introduced Communism into much of eastern Europe.

decathlon athletic contest made up of these ten different events for the competitor: 100 metres, long jump, shot-put, high jump, 400 metres, 110 metres hurdles, discus, pole vault, javelin, 1500 metres

defected left one country to live in another, without official permission

elfin small and attractive (like an elf)

endorsement declaration of approval for a product in return for money

media plural of medium (of communication), for example newspapers, magazines, TV and radio

Nazi short form of the National Socialist German Workers' Party, a political party led by Adolf Hitler

phenomenon remarkable person, thing or event

prodigy someone, especially a child, who is very talented

professional paid competitor

rationed when food and other materials are scarce, such as during and just after World War Two, they are distributed by an official system, so no one gets more than their share

repertoire the range of skills that a person has

rostrum victory platform

track and field sporting events which involve running, jumping, throwing and walking – such as the 100 metres or the javelin

USSR a Communist country, including Russia and many smaller nations, which broke up in 1991

Index